The Ascension Guide

Practical Advice for Lightworkers

LIA RUSS & MEGHMA HIRA

The Ascension Guide

Practical Advice for Lightworkers

SILVER PATH
PUBLISHING

For additional material related to this book, visit www.lightworkerslifeline.com.

The practices we discuss in the book are meant to enhance your understanding of yourself and the spiritual world. Think of them as spiritual tools. We do not represent that all of these methods will work for everyone. Therefore, we caution anyone against using them without supervision in any kind of dangerous situation. Always prioritize your physical, emotional, and mental safety.

Cover illustration and book design by Meghma Hira @ego.alchemist. Final typesetting by David J. Perry.

Body text set in Literata and Source Sans Pro, with headings in Vintage Moon and Dreaming Outloud.

Paperback edition   ISBN 979–8–9877045–2–3
E-book edition   ISBN 979–8–9877045–0–1

Contents

Introduction

PAST AND FUTURE

Lightworkers (Energy Workers, Healers, Seers, Mages, Shamans, Psychics, Empaths, Mediums, Mystics and others) have spent centuries hiding from the patriarchal religious and political authorities, who have wrongly proclaimed that our God-given gifts are somehow evil. We have been shunned, beaten, imprisoned, stoned and burned at the stake — all because, no matter how hard we tried to shut off our awarenesses, we could not. We were unable to ignore the stirrings of the full moon or the call of a bird. We could not stop being fed by being close to Nature or ignore Nature's ability to communicate with us. Mainstream society tried to frighten and shame us into the boxes that it wants everyone to fit in, and many of us, wishing to please, died trying to do so. Even if our bodies lived on, the pain we experienced daily, trying to exist cut off from the things that fed us, was torture.

It boggles the mind. We see things most people do not, we possess abilities and awarenesses that they do not ... but we do not look down on them, we do not diminish them, belittle, imprison or kill them. But they do us .... And yet, even though they have treated us this way for a millennium, we show up every day, as healers, each in our own way. Why is that? Are we perhaps aware of a grander scheme? What if ...?

What if God has had a master plan all along and it involved both humans being "made in God's image" — DIVINE — and being given free will? What if God was just waiting for us to get our heads out of our need to dominate, to quest for gold over God? In other words, God is waiting for us to get our heads out of our arsenal. Finding God means recognizing our Divinity and our interconnectedness. We are one in the soup of God ... no differences.

We are all one family, under God.

v

What if it had finally come to pass that enough of humanity has raised its eyes off the slop on the floor and has set its sights on the heavens? What if the call to Divinity in our cells has gotten too loud for us to ignore, and that level of awareness has flipped a switch? A switch that has turned the tide ... the tide of light versus dark. What if that flipped switch has also caused a corresponding awakening in "sleepers" on the planet? What might that look like?

Ascension!

Welcome to the future!

MAKING THE TRANSITION

After Lightworkers awaken, they cannot shut out awareness of the split between their inner world and outer reality, and things can quickly become overwhelming. The life that they worked so hard to create, the one where they attempted to awkwardly fit in and succeed, came at the expense of their inner reality and inner peace.

That by itself is uncomfortable, but when suddenly these walls come crumbling down ... you don't usually experience relief. You are mostly in shock. The conflict between inner awareness (which is now becoming stronger) and your lack of a relationship with it re-sults in your inner guidance not being able to inform you. This causes a lot of confusion and discomfort.

Now you can't go back, but you have no idea how to move forward. While you are at that crossroad, you also begin to experience a greater awareness of (sometimes disturbing) truths about our reality. We find ourselves compelled to see the darkness of an old energy that dominated our planet ... and at the same time, in order to survive this, we are equally compelled to find the light within ourselves.

Finding that light within is leading Lightworkers and old souls to recognize their Divinity. They learn about the true nature, power and benevolence of the Universe (and how to work with its magic and recognize miracles). Thanks to the internet and instant global communication, they are able to connect with other Lightworkers and learn to embrace their gifts and senses, as well as trust their inner wisdom and receive guidance from their Higher Selves.

Finally, you are called to a greater purpose, which may or may not be clear to you yet. You hear prophecies that those of us who awakened first agreed to be here at this special time in human history. You hear that we came here to break generational curses, dismantle the dysfunctional society, reconnect with nature, build abundance and herald the golden age of humanity.

For most of us, our initial reaction is … "Wow. That's a lot to take in." We might not feel up to the task; we may still be unclear what our part is in this miraculous production. This is where we will tell you to take a deep breath — you are exactly where you need to be, at precisely the right time. In this new paradigm we need to live in our hearts, where we can feel the flow of life all around us, and from where we can feel our guidance. We are being called to grow into ourselves and follow our inner promptings (often as the result of so much speaking to us, or through us).

This book will be your friend and confidant through your ascension journey, guiding you in your exploration of yourself and this new reality. It shows you how to protect yourself and how to ground. It illustrates the pitfalls and drawbacks you may encounter on your journey as well as methods for dealing with these. It encourages you to find your inner truths and listen to them.

ABOUT THIS BOOK

Inside these pages you will find the combined 70 years' experience of Lia and Meghma. Their knowledge spans East and West, modern and ancient, natural and scientific. They have been witnessing an unprecedented number of people waking up, as if stepping out of the movie *The Matrix*.

A primer is needed, and if any such book ever existed, it has disappeared from our knowledge. We have created such a book (the one you are holding) to help answer many of the most common questions newly awakened Lightworkers ask, as well as provide information that is important for them to have that they may not be aware of.

This book was put together to help Lightworkers raise and maintain high vibrations as they discover and experience their incredible journeys. In it we explain over ten Lightworker self-care modalities. These are drawn from the spiritual/energetic practices that have helped us the most to cope and thrive in the current times of change.

DEDICATION

This is book is dedicated in honor of all Lightworkers who are on Earth right now, overcoming challenges, shining their light, healing the planet, and leading the collective. We wish to remind whoever reads *The Ascension Guide: Practical Advice for Lightworkers* that you are not alone in this journey. We are all reaching out and looking out for each other.

We see you!

ACKNOWLEDGMENT
We also are eternally grateful to our editor David Perry for his ability to perform not only the role of editor, but that of mentor and friend as well. He has given our words wings so that they may reach beyond our own spheres … a gift that is unparalleled in our lives.
Thank you David!

What Is Ascension?

The ascension journey is both an individual endeavor and a collective quest. The amount of light available to us is increasing (remember that light is a much higher vibration than matter). As more light bathes our physical bodies, it interacts with us, causing a quickening. For those who have been preparing for this, the internal shift we are required to make to adjust to these changes can be almost overwhelming. When the increasing frequencies start to shift people who have not prepared for this, it can be too much for them. This is one of the reasons so many are choosing to leave the planet now.

As we hold more light within ourselves and embody our divine essence, we are also shifting planetary consciousness.

Each one of us has the ability to tune into an inner knowing. From here we will be able to identify our gifts and get a sense of how we are to work with them. This has always been so. What is new now is that all Lightworkers are experiencing a quickening, simultaneously, for the purpose of working together in an unprecedented way, for the first time in the history of the planet.

In 2012 when the Mayan calendar ended, instead of spiraling into war and unconsciousness, we entered into a new level of consciousness. This sent us into a new timeline, one where the old paradigm ended. Although old souls have not experienced this in past lifetimes, there is now more light on the planet than darkness. This is fabulous news, and its reality will become more and more apparent as time passes. Please note that there are still pockets of deep darkness and the wielders of that darkness are not going to give up their domains easily, without a fight. But the truth is, darkness is not active. If you open a door to a dark room from a brightly lit hall, what happens? Does darkness rush into the hall? Or does light rush into the darkness?

All we need to do is continue to learn how to hold and channel our light. And darkness must flee before us!

If you have not experienced this yet, do not worry. The more you practice tuning into all your systems for reading and interacting with energy, the clearer your path will become.

What You May Be Experiencing

Common symptoms of Awakening and Ascension are:

- Disturbances in sleep patterns (sleeping too little or too much, waking up at odd hours)

- Dietary shifts

- Seeing Angel Numbers and other synchronicities

- Ringing and/or pressure in ears

- Dissatisfaction with prior social circles & lifestyle

- Altered tolerance for many things (light, noise, etc.)

- Increase in sensitivities

- Decreased ability to deal with lower vibrations

- Inner demand to change careers

- Flu-like symptoms

- Aversion toward news and mass media

- Purging

- Fuzzy thinking or difficulty thinking

- Headaches

- Fatigue

- Overwhelm

- Experiencing variations in energy levels, up and down

- Feeling drawn to be in nature

- Desire to isolate, even when feeling lonely

- Unexplained anxiety, fear and/or depression

On a More Positive Note

Common signs of Awakening and Ascension include:

- Heightened awareness
- Heightened sensitivities
- Increase in any pre-existing gifts
- Experiencing new gifts
- Discovering one's soul family
- Discovering one's soul purpose
- Getting back in touch with one's inner child
- Greater ability to feel connections
- Greater ability to manifest
- Releasing old fears and addictions
- Connecting with (inner and higher) guidance
- Greater ability to feel our connection to Source
- Living with authenticity and power
- Opening and expanding our hearts to love & abundance
- Spontaneous rushes of energy, joy, bliss

Younger Starseeds and Lightworkers who are waking up now feel confused and disoriented, as they become unplugged from the system that supported the old paradigm (which has died — but will be going through its death throes for a while). Finding ourselves unplugged, before the new paradigm is fully formed, is scary because we are being asked to create the new paradigm as we go. It can feel impossible; a true leap of faith is required to let go of the old before we can even see clearly where we want to land. All we know for sure is that we need change — we feel this screaming inside us.

For older Starseeds and Lightworkers, there was no internet, no way to determine that others were going through similar things. We were alone, doing the best we could to hold onto our light while we were inundated by an entire world that shut us out, told us we were crazy or tried to eat up our light.

We devised methods for surviving, which often meant trying to hide our light, even from ourselves. If we could not resist the call of our souls to work our healing gifts in the world, we discovered that we needed strong methods to protect ourselves.

This fact alone caused harm to sensitive Lightworkers. This long lasting paradigm caused serious layers of trauma and blockages that older Lightworkers now need to consciously shed.

Please know your suffering has not been in vain! The paradigm has shifted, the light quota on this planet has increased exponentially. All gifts are expanding, but we must learn how to operate in the new paradigm. There are too many changes to cover here, and often the changes are apparent to different lightworkers in unique ways.

This is why we need to learn the subtle sensory language that exists when we connect to Source or utilize any of our biological systems for reading and working with energy.

What is amazing is that any of us survived in these circumstances. But we did and we have paved the way to make it easier for the rest to come. We are all needed so desperately now, to build our light, to realize our unity.

We are no longer alone. Among those who are reading this are beautiful and wise souls who grew up feeling that they must be here by mistake. We have experienced that feeling of constant unease and a deeper knowing that something ought to be different.

There will come a day when people of all races, colors, and creeds will put aside their differences. They will come together in love, joining hands in unification, to heal the Earth and all Her children.

- NAVAJO-HOPI PROPHECY

Definitions

There may be terms we use in the book that you are unfamiliar with. We have created a list of short descriptions here. If you would like to see our full list of definitions, please visit our website, https://lightworkerslifeline.com/home/glossary/

ANGEL NUMBERS
Vibrational information, guidance from our Spirit Team, energetic information, and/or synchronicities expressed in the form of repeating numbers.

CLAIRS
All of the spiritual or psychic ways humans are able to be aware of, interpret, generate or move energy through various systems within the body. These abilities are studied under the umbrella of extra-sensory perception (ESP) and are commonly referred to as 'clairs.' There are five types of clairs: clairvoyance, clairsentience, clairaudience, claircognizance, and clairolfactance (or clairalience).

MANIFESTATION
Creating a real physical experience from imagination, belief and thought through consistent affirmations and aligned actions.

MASTER NUMBERS
A special group of angel numbers in which the same numeral is repeated two or more times, such that they are also multiples of 11.

MULTIDIMENSIONS
Realities existing and operating beyond our linear perception of space, time and energy.

MULTIDIMENSIONAL BEING
A corporeal being who accesses or interacts with realities beyond the three-dimensional space-time.

PLASMA
The fourth fundamental state of matter (the first three are solid, liquid, and gas). Plasma is characterized by high concentrations of charged particles (electrons and ions).

QUANTUM FIELD
An energetic field of infinite possibilities created by vibrating sub-atomic particles that respond to consciousness.

STARSEEDS
Souls from other star systems who are incarnating on Earth as humans to plant the seeds of higher consciousness within the collective.

SYNCHRONICITY
An external event that confirms an internal belief.

Notes

Energetic Cleansing

Just the way you need to clean your physical house, office, car, or body, the energy fields of these need to be cleansed as well. This can be done using a variety of techniques and materials that we will cover in this chapter.

TIMES FOR ENERGETIC CLEANSING

When we have a challenging day or an argument with a loved one or co-worker, these are important times to incorporate an EC (Energy Cleansing) ritual.

When we purchase a new crystal or bring an older object into our homes, doing an EC helps ensure that no un-wanted outside energy enters your space via such objects.

News of war and plague, gossip, pro-cessed food, noise, and air pollution — all these lower our natural frequency. Regularly cleansing the energetic field around us can be a huge help in making space for the higher frequencies to keep pouring in.

ENERGETIC REVOLUTION

We are in an energetic revolution! The remarkable aspect of participating in this revolution is that it is mostly an in-side job! Cleaning up our emotional waters will help the planet as much as separating our household waste does.

Smudging

Smudging is the act of burning a sacred herb, oil, resin, or wood to produce smoke in which one bathes a body, object, or place to cleanse it of unwelcome energies.

It is believed in many traditions that smoke enters the spirit realm. Consequently, burning a cleansing herb is believed to remove negativity from the spirit realm.

But smudging has an effect on other things as well. For instance, scientists have tested the percentage of bacteria in a room before and after burning sage in it. They found that burning sage lowers the presence of harmful bacteria in the surrounding atmosphere for up to two weeks.

So there are many reasons to burn sacred herbs. And it is interesting that our ancestors, without the aid of modern scientific equipment, were able to discern not only how to do this, but which herbs worked for this purpose as well.

This was accomplished by sensitives, who were (and *are*) able to discern such things and more. This is what we want to help you achieve.

CLEANSING HERBS

Before we move into the technique of smudging, we would like to introduce you to some common cleansing herbs that can be burned to cleanse the energy of a room, object, or person.

Sage (sagebrush or plateau sage) a type of artemisia found in the southwestern United States, was used for cleansing by many Native American nations for thousands of years. However, in recent years, white sage, a type of salvia which grows in California, has replaced traditional sage in stores and so is the one most people in the USA are familiar with.

A lesser-known herb, mugwort, which grows prolifically in the northeastern USA, and has been used for this purpose by people from this region.

In South America, the aromatic wood of the palo santo tree is used for energetic cleansing and has spread in popularity around the world. Leaves from the bael tree (Bengal quince or *aegle marmelos*) are also burned during fire rites for their cleansing properties.

Also, although herbs like sage are often sold in large bundles (called smudge wands or sticks), you do not need to burn that much material all at once, and doing so can actually be overwhelming. Opening the bundle and burning a single leaf is often sufficient to cleanse a large house.

If you do not have access to any of the traditional ingredients, then use your intuition to guide you. Choose an incense and clear the area or object by focusing on your intention to do so and the smoke of what you have chosen. Believe it or not, that can be enough.

Always check in after any cleansing to "see" if the object, person, or space feels better. If it doesn't, you can smudge again, or use another method that we will describe in the following chapters.

RESINS AND OILS

For thousands of years, people have used natural resins such as:

- Frankincense (*olibanum*) made from Boswellia trees
- Myrrh, produced from Commiphora trees that grow in India, northeast Asia and the Arabian Peninsula
- Copal, from trees typically found in Mexico, Central and South America.

In traditional Indian households, fragrant natural resins are mixed with dried coconut husks and burned to keep bugs and negative energies at bay.

Please do not use resins or oils from trees like Boswellia if you can find more renewable / sustainable herbs such as sage and other herbaceous plants.

HOW TO SMUDGE

To cleanse an object, simply hold it in the smoke of your choice. If it is too big to hold in the stream of smoke, you can use your hands to catch or push the smoke in the desired direction.

A single feather or a fan made from many feathers or sacred herbs may be used for directing the smoke as well. In India, Nepal, and Tibet, yak hair is attached to a scepter-like handle (called a chamara) and is used instead of a fan for this purpose.

As the smoke washes over the item, ask all discordant energies to leave and harmonious energies to flow in.

See how this feels. Some teachings say that once you clear energy out of some-place, you should take care to replace it with specifically intended energies. (The universe abhors a vacuum and will fill it with what is available.) So you may want to choose which energy replaces the one you just asked to leave. This can be done using your intentions or by burning a different invocational herb.

For example, the Lakota consider sweetgrass to be an herb that is pleasing to positive spirits, so after burning sage to clear an area of negative energies they will burn sweetgrass to invite in positive ones. You also see examples of this in the Catholic church with various substances burned in the thuribles borne by altar servers.

Sound

Sound is made up of frequencies which can be very useful in energetic cleansing; they are able to break down unwanted structures in physical, mental, emotional and spiritual bodies.

Humans have one of the most extraordinary voice boxes in nature. Sounds made within the body (using breath and vocalization) can be used in all four above-mentioned cases to remove unwanted energies.

Sacred sounds (or frequencies) can be used for clearing and balancing the chakras and organs in our bodies. Since there are specific frequencies at which individual organs thrive or heal, these frequencies can be used to help an ailing part of the body vibrate at the optimum level for health.

Furthermore, sound can cleanse physical objects and spaces. Simply place an object on a surface and direct sound towards it. Traditional instruments for this purpose include drums, rattles, wind instruments, gongs, chimes, bells, singing bowls, tuning forks, and of course the voice.

You can easily get your own singing bowls and tuning forks to use in your sound cleansing rituals, or play 417Hz (a frequency known for removing negative energy). Alternatively, you can clap loudly or bang some pots, rocks or

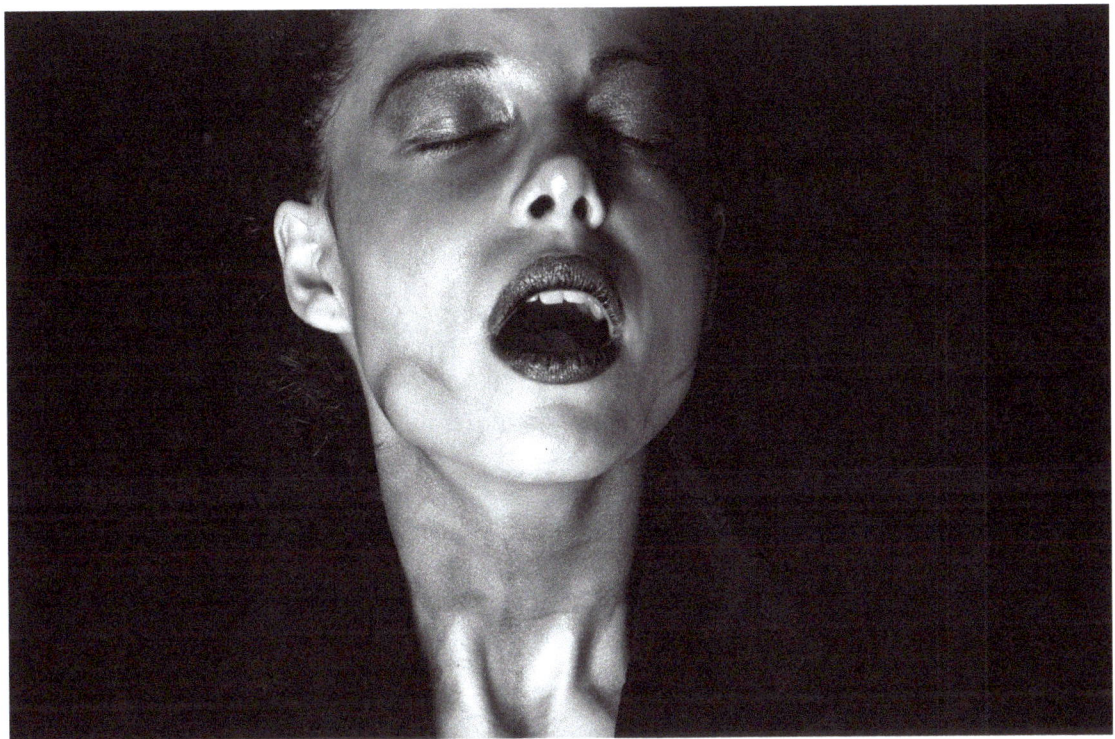

sticks together and ask the "bad spirits" to leave your house. Many ancient cultures used sound to drive away negative energies or spirits.

Unlike smoke, we cannot see sound, but we can be aware of its passing through the air, as several of our biological systems are designed for registering vibrational frequencies.

Note: sound waves are very powerful. When using anything other than your voice, it is paramount to be sensitive to the quality and intensity of the vibrations you use.

The sounds we make reverberate through our skeletal structures and reach every cell, neuron, and synapse. Producing a deep humming sound at the base of your throat and moving the vibration around and outward from your body can shift the energies instantaneously.

Salt

The use of salt for cleansing and protecting goes back at least a thousand years. It might be the only magical commodity that is so readily available, although it was once very expensive.

There are many methods for using salt for cleansing. One way is to submerge or stand an object in dry salt. This is safest for other minerals and some crystals which should not be placed in liquid.

A second method is to dissolve salt in water and submerge your object. Do your research here; some minerals are toxic if absorbed through the skin. Immersing any of these in a salty solution (or any liquid) can cause it to become dangerous, whereas handled dry it is relatively harmless.

Remember that water holds the vibration of our thoughts, so be sure to in- clude your intentions in this process. You can also consecrate and bless the salt water to enhance its properties be- fore use.

More Methods for Cleansing

Historically, different cultures developed many creative ways to cleanse the energy of objects, people and spaces. Elders often say it is important to learn the way your ancestors did things. So do some exploring. Use your intuition in these matters as not all such traditions may be appropriate for every situation (or material).

In addition to smoke, sound, and salt, you can use running water, Florida water, wind, rain, sunlight, moonlight and fire for cleansing rituals.

For those who cannot create or are allergic to smoke, Florida water or a spray made from sage or crystals known for their cleansing properties can be used.

If you wish to use only your intentions, a prop like a crystal or a knife to focus your energy may be used. Or you may just utilize the light of your focused awareness. You can state, "All negative energies must transmute to positive energies. Any energy that does not wish to be transmuted must leave." If you feel the need, you can add "and never return."

Also be sure to check in with how the object, person,or place feels to you before and after. If you are still feeling uncomfortable, raise your own personal shield and add prayers.

This should work in most cases. But, if you are still feeling uncomfortable, don't hesitate to reach out for help.

Notes

Grounding Techniques

Almost everyone can benefit from grounding (or earthing). Today we hear about two kinds of grounding, one where we must have physical contact with the bare earth (earthing), and the more traditional concept of grounding attained through creative visualizations, intentions and certain kinds of meditation.

Regarding earthing, it is said that, because we wear shoes with soles of man-made materials, our energy cannot ground into the earth. It is also said that the earth cannot connect to us as well. Our electromagnetic systems benefit from skin contact with the earth because of her natural electric charge.

This charge has been proven to stabilize the functioning of our bodies on a cellular level, reducing inflammation, pain and stress, while improving blood flow, energy and sleep.

In contrast, traditional grounding is achieved by visualizing a cord of light coming from the base of your spine and going deep into the earth. Some people imagine this cord going into a beautiful crystal at the center of the earth. Some imagine being a part of the Great Tree whose roots go deep into the earth. You can imagine the same for your feet if it feels appropriate. Don't be afraid to experiment. This practice helps with being spacey, disoriented, lightheaded, unfocused, dizzy, jittery, anxious, irritable, indecisive and forgetful. Grounding also has been shown to improve immune function and promote better sleep.

For Lightworkers and possibly more so for Starseeds (who can feel a general disconnect from the planet), grounding can be considered an essential part of basic daily hygiene and self-care. So much of what we do requires us to open our upper chakras and energy centers to connect with our Higher Self and beyond. This can leave us unbalanced unless we consciously ground ourselves each time. Grounding can also be used as needed, but keep in mind that we often ignore our own self-care, and a regular practice can leave us in a better place to deal with what life throws at us.

Furthermore, connecting to natural objects or other living bodies can also ground and calm us. Everything that lives on, within, or soars above the planet is deeply connected to Gaia. By focusing on an aspect of her and opening ourselves (all of our awareness and senses) to Gaia, we are able to connect with her. Through this connection, we can not only learn of her essence, energy, and medicine, but we are also able to ground ourselves.

The next three sections show how to use different aspects of Gaia to help you ground and anchor your energies to the earth's magnetic grid.

Grounding helps us not be too scattered. It helps us stay focused and supports our bodies if our own energies become stretched too thin.

Our Beloved Earth

The moon affects human consciousness when it passes closest to us in it's monthly cycle.
The Earth is much lager and its
electromagnetic field is directly below our feet every day.
Is it reasonable to think her
field does not affect us (as the
current paradigm maintains)?
Would it be more reasonable to
assume that the force the
Earth exerts on us would be
much greater? And so it is.

Some say that our electromagnetic fields are interwoven
with that of the Earth, and this
makes sense. Given out prox-
imity to the Earth and her
mass, it would be impossible
for our electromagnetic fields
to be completely separate.

Since the invention of rubber soles,
which cut off our electromagnetic field
from the Earth (think about how rubber tires prevent lightning from flow-
ing through a metal car into its human
occupants), many diseases of the mind
and body have become much more
prevalent. And not just in humans; the
Earth herself is also suffering.

Exploring our connections with the
Earth is grounding in and of itself. Sit
on the ground. Take your shoes and
socks off if you can; even better, dig
your feet into the dirt. Breathe deeply
and feel the Earth's negative ions
pulling all the things that no longer
serve you out of the the soles of your
feet. Imagine a taproot extending out

of the base of your spine; see it reaching deep into the Earth. If you like, see it connecting to a glorious crystal at the center of the Earth.

Doing this for just ten to fifteen minutes will bring remarkable changes in your energies. You will feel lighter and brighter. Practicing this daily will change your life.

If you do not have daily access to a natural space to connect with Gaia, then you can hold your favorite crystal, a potted plant, or a root vegetable from your pantry to call in the energy and healing of Mother Gaia.

Trees

According to the Quechua people, humans are walking trees. We alone among all other creatures walk erect on two legs, which resemble tree trunks (and our torso is often referred to as a trunk). Like the branches on a tree, we have arms and fingers.

Trees are our benefactors in many ways. Without wood, our lives would be very different. Trees supply materials to build out shelters. They also make possible the fires we use to warm ourselves and cook our food.

Beyond creature comforts, trees provide medicines, like the willow (aspirin) and the cinchona (quinine).

Trees communicate with each other and (believe it or not) with us. With their deep-reaching roots, trees are profoundly grounded in the Earth. Sitting beneath a tree, or hugging one and opening our senses to it, can allow us to feel what the tree is experiencing. By doing so we take in the template for that grounded peace, and it becomes available for us to step into afterwards, any time we remember it.

Trees are intelligent and sentient beings. They are patient, social, and cooperative. Old trees that outlived generations of humans stand silently holding within themselves eons of knowledge and wisdom.

Our breathing is linked cyclically to trees. They create oxygen which we consume, while we exhale carbon dioxide as a waste product which they take in and utilize. Exploring that cycle can be helpful in connecting more deeply to trees.

Trees emit large amounts of phytochemicals to cleanse themselves. These help humans in many ways. For instance, one of the phytochemicals that cedar trees give off affects our nervous system. A two-hour exposure to this one phytochemical will lower a person's blood pressure for up to two weeks — with no negative side effects!

James Redfield says that one of the best ways to get energy is to pick a tree that you are drawn to and spend ten minutes a day appreciating it. He says this creates a bio-feedback loop of positive energy that will enhance our lives.

Get a tree-pal today! Sitting barefoot under a strong, big tree or leaning against it is one of the most comforting things to a spiritually inclined human.

Have you hugged a tree today?

24

Crystals

The molecular structure of a crystal determines its shape and whether it is a ruby, emerald, diamond, quartz, etc. (as well as its color). The shape of a crystal greatly affects its frequencies, as does its color.

You can work with crystals and stones using the properties of their molecular structure. For example, to balance or ground your root chakra, you could work with any naturally occurring red stones. The color red is a frequency of light, and it matches the frequency of the root chakra when the latter is balanced.

You can also work with crystals and stones according to their energetic properties. These may be determined by anyone skilled in opening and attuning themselves to a stone. For example, hematite's natural properties render it a perfect stone for grounding, and this can be felt by those who are sensitive.

Quartz, on the other hand, is well known to amplify or hold steady whatever frequencies are around it (depending on its temperature). So you would not use quartz crystals to ground, especially if you were already in an ungrounded state. In this situation try placing a stone used for grounding on the quartz crystal (thus making use of the latter's amplifying properties).

Initially, it is best to follow tried and true information (there are a lot of false claims in circulation created to sell products, even stones). Once you have a good understanding of the basics of sensing and directing energy, protecting yourself, creating boundaries, cleansing, and what it feels like to send and receive energy from your centers, you can experiment on your own.

I have heard it said that crystals are the highest expression of the Earth's imagination. They certainly are exquisite to look at!

Just as with a tarot deck, the visual points of interest within or on the surface of a crystal can speak to us. This intuitive "conversation" can often lead to a download of new information. Sim-

ply gaze at the crystal and explore its inner and outer terrain. Allow the mind and heart to open as you do this. Notice how you feel. Pay attention to any information that you may receive. After doing this for 10 minutes, see if you are feeling more grounded and centered in your being.

When you are new to crystals, it is good to get a crystal guidebook (or teacher) that is grounded in solid information. Here are two of our favorites:

- *Love Is in the Earth* by Melody will give you an excellent foundation in the traditional uses of crystals.
- *The Book of Stones* by Robert Simmons and Naisha Ahsian is an excellent book that covers more unusual crystals and minerals from two different perspectives.

Notes

Notes

Lightbody Conditioning

Lightworkers are beings of light. With conscious tending of our inner gardens (or any other metaphor that resonates with you), we will produce more and more of this precious commodity — "Let there be light!" Fear is the only thing that diminishes our light. What makes it grow? Take a look at the following list for ideas. You will notice that these are, for the most part, activities that feel good to the individual. In other words, pursuing bliss enhances your ability to grow your light (and raise your vibration). It sounds simple, but many Lightworkers have been conditioned to shy away from self-care or self-indulgence. This may be one of our biggest hurdles to overcome.

Ways to strengthen our ability to shine include the following:

- Love
- Joy
- Self-expression (speaking our truth, dancing, singing, being creative, moving, eating well, etc.)
- Peace
- Feeling safe
- Gratitude
- Meditation
- Connection
- Movement (Yoga, stretching, wandering, Tai Chi, martial arts and Qi Gong)
- Hydration and sleep

Conscious Movement

Our bodies are designed to move. Movement can be a form of meditation, a prayer, an ecstatic expression of our inner being, or something that our heads tell us to do.

In our modern culture, we constantly get confused by the blanket statement that "bigger is better." So we believe that we have to exercise really hard, or cover a lot of ground, or keep it up for long periods of time in order for exercise to benefit us.

But it is not the only truth.

Small movements, repeated just ten times, once or several times a day, can bring tone back to almost every part of our body.

Tone is an expression of a kind of unity we can share with our bodies. It almost seems as if our bodies respond to our focused -attention as much as they do to physical exercise.

Deepening our connection to our bodies allows us to tap into the wisdom that resides within the body. We thereby create a necessary alliance, which strengthens not only all our gifts, but our ability to be powerful Lightworkers as well.

I have found the more tone I have in my muscles, the more easily I can feel energy in them.

Much exploration needs to be done in this area, especially as we move into the new paradigm. But we have definitely determined that our bodies are magnificent devices for working with energy. We have also determined that in many areas the body's innate wisdom far outshines our intellect.

Begin to embody your soul more fully. Allow yourself to be guided by movements your body wants to make, sounds your body longs to utter. Give yourself permission to be guided by the whisperings (or screams) of your inner guidance. Dance, walk, sing, stretch, or scream in nature; all of these will help you re-home your consciousness into your body.

There are so many ways to connect more deeply with your body. Being led by what feels good to you or what brings you pleasure or joy is a great way to start.

Learn Yoga, Qi Gong, Tai Chi — it really doesn't matter which. Every body is different. Just move.

Breathwork

How we breathe communicates so much to our bodies. Bringing awareness to our breath can connect us more deeply with our bodies and bring us back to conscious presence.

Our breathing also affects the amount of Ki (Qi) or Prana we are taking in from our lungs. Small shallow breaths constrict our energy and communicate fear to our bodies. Slow, deep breathing allows the body to enter a calmer state. The state of your body affects the ways you are able to work with energy, especially in the beginning.

Another self-check-in practice is to observe the present flow of your breath and communicate with it. If it is rapid, uneven, or shallow, you may want to pay special attention to what it is trying to tell you or what it needs from you.

Experiment with this awareness. How do the various types of breathing mentioned above affect you?

FOUR-PART BREATHING
Four-part breathing is an excellent method for resetting your stress levels and also for grounding. To practice this technique, take a deep breath in as you count to four, hold your breath for another count of four, exhale to the count of four, and for the last step hold for the count of four. Repeat this for a

couple of rounds. Then go back to normal breathing and take note of how you feel.

Which stage in this process is most comfortable for you? Which place is hardest? Do any of them bring a sense of fear (constriction)? Do any of them bring a sense of expansiveness and connection to something greater than yourself? None of these responses is better or worse than the others. They are all just information for you to work with.

Practice four-part breathing anytime you are feeling anxious or stressed. Also try it before you do energy work and see if anything changes. Write down your discoveries.

THE LONG EXHALE
Another technique that works wonders in the event of an anxious episode is to do a very long exhale. All you have to do is take a slow deep breath and then pucker your lips slightly (like you are learning to whistle) and exhale out all the air from your lungs through the small gap between your lips before taking in your next breath. This ensures that we exhale more slowly than we inhale and is effective in calming heart palpitations and racing thoughts. This method can also help you to maintain focus and clarity during work.

Some breathwork can be learned by simply observing our bodies' natural intelligence.

Have you ever noticed that when you are sad or disappointed, you sigh deeply and more often? This is your body using breath to release the stress or emotions of that moment.

To emulate this bodily wisdom, take a long, deep breath and exhale through the mouth with a breathy "Ha!" sound. This helps let go of thoughts and emotions that are weighing us down.

Conscious Eating

Since one of our goals is to deepen our conscious connection with the beautiful instruments we are born in, fueling and taking good care of that precious "ride" is important. The type of fuel we need varies depending on many factors, one of which is your level of connection to your body.

At this moment, what does your body need? It often will not need the same thing all the time. Therefore the greater your connection with your body, the better your understanding of its specific needs, and consequently, the better a team you make.

With excellent teamwork, many things barely dreamed of are possible. But if your connection is tenuous (or even adversarial), then what you crave may be very different than what your ride wants or needs.

For example, if you are an emotional eater, when you crave comfort, you may feel drawn to eat moist chocolate cake with a thick, rich dark chocolate frosting. Sugar can be bad for many bodies, especially if you have diabetes or an overgrowth of yeast. Eating sugar might make you feel soothed emotionally but make your body feel unwell.

INNER DISCERNMENT
Everything begins with learning to tune into the nuances of the communi-

cations you receive from your earthly vehicle. The level (mastery) of communication between us and our body allow us to be ultra-aware of energetic shifts. This level of awareness is one of the ways we communicate non-verbally with other beings.

It is vitally important to learn to interpret nuances in our dietary preferences. For example, when candida (or candidiasis) reaches a significant population in our body, it is able to communicate directly with the brain. Its language is chemical, therefore it is simple and effective. The parasite sends chemical instructions to our brain demanding what it needs to survive: sugar, starches, and carbs. As this information originates from within us, we may not understand that our brain is being fooled into these powerful cravings. It can be virtually impossible to discern that these cravings are not ours.

However, if one is able to cut out the majority of foods the yeast craves (most importantly, sugar), its numbers dwindle rapidly and so does that craving for sugar and sweetened food.

This is why there cannot be a one-sized diet that fits all. For some, it may become important to lessen or even cut out meat from their diets. For those whose sugar cravings rule, try agave syrup. It tastes the closest to sugar

(having virtually no taste of its own) and it does not support yeast. Stevia is a good alternative as well, although it does have a taste (which is hard to describe). Switch to fruit instead of processed sugars. As with everything, let your body guide you.

Many of us are discovering that our need for food and the types of food are changing. Tune into your body. Form an alliance with it. Work together towards your greater good. You could have no better companion more aligned with your success. The goal is to have a lighter body (not necessarily in weight) but with high energy and confidence to do the things that you love.

As many of you are working with your third eye (pineal gland), it will serve you well to keep in mind that fluoride (found in both municipal water sources and many brands of toothpaste) is said to calcify and block this gland/energy center. Also, note that excessive (or frequent) alcohol consumption can weaken your ability to work with this energy as well.

Again, these are general guidelines. Listening to your body and inner guidance is an excellent practice to augment any external guidance or diet advice.

INNATE
The consciousness of our cellular structure has been referred to as "Innate." Innate has much wisdom; it is what tells our cells how to heal a cut or knit a broken bone.

Our hearts beat over 100,000 times each day without our ever thinking about it. Our lungs take in oxygen and exchange it for waste gases in our bodies… all without our focusing on it.

Forming an alliance with Innate's intelligence is wise, and not something we are encouraged to do. We are taught instead that the physical body has no knowledge beyond "instinct," an impulse followed blindly with no intelligence in it. And so we are in essence taught to disrespect not just our bodies, but all bodies in our universe.

So how do we put the power of Innate into our daily lives and align with it?

The first step to building a relationship with Innate is to cultivate self-love and respect for our bodies. Contemplating how much our bodies endure and work for us (and focusing on being grateful) will open a door to connecting consciously to Innate's vast intelligence and complexity.

This bonding or alliance with Innate can be very helpful in overcoming many disorders, from eating to sleeping to drug addictions or misuse of our sexual energy.

The most basic yet effective way to communicate with our Innate wisdom is through verbalized commands. When we enunciate our thoughts in the form of speech, we create vibrations in the air around us. Our bodies have many sensitive receptors that recognize these frequencies. So when you say out loud, "I am healthy, wealthy and wise," your cellular structure hears you and does everything in its power to match that.

You can ask Innate for guidance in many areas of your life, including what you should eat. Our dysfunctional heads will have us eating all manner of things that do not serve our body. Innate will never do this. Who's a better friend to listen to? The choice as always is yours. I know what my answer to that question is!

Notes

Channeling Guidance

Channeling can be an odd concept if you have never experienced it. It is even an odd experience when it is occurring. Having information downloaded into you head can produce a tingling or mild tickling sensation. For some it is less of a sensation and more a sense of having entered a different space-time dimension (often sensed as a space that exists above your head, either directly, slightly in front or behind). Within this space it is possible to see or understand information and both integrate it and bring it with you when you leave. You may have a different experience. Becoming aware of the accompanying sensations/awarenesses

will help you identify and work with this process.

If you are not grounded when this is occurring, you can really get spacey and disoriented. It can be incredibly difficult to focus on anything or even string sentences together properly. This is one of the reasons it is so important to understand when we are dealing with side effects caused by our gifts, as opposed to experiencing mental, emotional or physical illness.

One can channel anything, from receiving information (answers, cures or guidance) to being a conduit for a disembodied spirit to speak through.

Some well known examples of channeled spirits are Kryon, Abraham Hicks, Adoranda, Seth and Emmanuel. Marilyn Harper, who channels Adoranda, says:

"Everyone channels slightly differently! Sometimes it's through lyrics, art, music, spoken word, numbers, or writing."

How do you know if you can trust channeled information or channeled entities? The same way you would a person. Don't believe anything they say initially, or at least not everything.

Get to know them over time. Use your other gifts of discernment, heart knowing or intuition. Pay attention to how you feel as you listen to them; do you feel uplifted, honored for exactly where you are? Does what you are hearing resonate inside you in a pleasant or exciting way? Or do you feel diminished, admonished, corrected, less than, or afraid? Interestingly, it is much easier to cause someone to feel afraid or diminished than it is to make them feel good, at peace, loved or safe. So chances are, if you are feeling any of those positive things, you are in good hands, so to speak.

Journaling

Keeping a journal will be a valuable tool on your journey to the center of yourself, and from there out into the multi-dimensional universe. Since this is an inward journey first, keeping of experiments and their outcomes will be invaluable information.

Remember that in this realm information is power.

But this information is quite likely unique to you. There may be significance revealed that you do not recognize at first. We often need to hear something many times before it "clicks" for us. Keeping a journal ensures that all the messages or information you receive remains accessible to you as you become ready for it.

You may want to divide your journal into sections each day: for example, Dreams, Intentions for the Day, Moon Phase, Ascension Symptoms Experienced, Astrological Events, Notes, Discoveries and a Gratitude List.

We have a Journal Template for you to copy and print out if you like. Go to https://lightworkerslifeline.com/home/journal-template/

Divination

Even when we are not aware of our connection to the creative Source of all, it is still aware of us. How could it not be, when we carry its divine spark (or more) within us?

So we are never alone. Never. All we need do is look around us for signs — they are everywhere.

What about synchronistic occurrences or angel numbers? What might be the meaning of each one? Lean into them. Explore the nuances and discover what message is hidden within, for your eyes/ears only.

If you are an old soul (as most Lightworkers are), there is so much you can pick up from going within and learning the subtle non-verbal language used here.

Would it surprise you to know that the best tarot card readers use the established meanings of each card only minimally? It's true. The best ones open up to communication from different sources (intuition, Higher Self, ancestors, guides, angels, and other multidimensional beings) to get specific messages or information in a reading.

For example, readers will consciously notice (be drawn to) one feature from the card that doesn't usually catch their attention. They lean into that image, and new information comes to

ORACLE CARD READING

When you are first starting, getting an oracle deck may be the easiest form of divination to work with. Since each oracle deck is completely different (unlike tarot which has defined cards with a hierarchy and meaning), no one expects you to memorize the intended meaning of each card.

One way to work with an oracle is simply to shuffle the deck with a question in your mind. After a minute, fan the deck or spread the cards out on a flat surface and pick one. Sometimes it will be appropriate to pick more than one card (some might "call to you," drawing your attention, while others may fall (or jump) out of the deck as you shuffle or are pulling out the cards of your choice. Pulling cards for guidance can be done daily, weekly, or more sporadically. It depends on your need.

them. They then temper that information with the universal meaning of the card and its placement in the reading. This form of divination takes trust and practice.

We can use this method of opening ourselves to speak with our inner guidance and apply it to other areas of our lives.

Tarot and oracle cards, the runes, and other divination tools are all great ways to gain clarity on what you are being guided to focus on at a given time.

Allow yourself to be guided.

WORKING WITH TAROT

Using tarot cards for divination is very similar to using oracle cards. The major difference is that, unlike oracle decks, tarot decks are divided into two parts. The Major Arcana contains 22 cards that represent bigger themes and energies in our lives while the Minor Arcana contains 56 cards divided into four suits, much like common playing cards.

Each tarot card has an associated number, element, and standard meaning that help in getting insightful and detailed readings. However, the illustrations on the cards vary from deck to deck and the images open up avenues for deeper exploration.

Tarot cards can be read either using specific spreads (of 2, 3, 5, 11, or more cards) or by drawing them intuitively from the deck or while shuffling. Once you have your cards for the reading, you can tune into the messages they convey.

Can you see a story being told by the cards in front of you?

The easiest way to become proficient in oracle or tarot readings is to do a reading for yourself every other day. This simple practice can help build a deep relationship with your Higher Self and spirit guides while priming you to be channels of higher wisdom and truth. Soon, it will feel like having a daily chat with your cosmic support system.

OTHER DIVINATION METHODS

Many things may be used for scrying and for developing communication skills between your mind and your various types of inner knowing, such as intuition and discernment. In addition to oracle and tarot cards, these tools include:

- Crystals (natural)
- Crystal balls
- Runes
- Tea leaves
- Wax
- Eggs
- Bones
- Mirrors
- A bowl or pool of water
- A reflective object
- Animal or insect behaviors
- Stars and planets

Meditation

It used to be that meditation involved long hours of sitting in lotus position, struggling to keep your posture erect and your mind blank. While that worked for certain people, many others found it foreign or offputting. That practice resonated more with the old paradigm, which idealizes the mind and put much of its energy into cutting individuals off from their innate spiritual power.

Today, Wikipedia says of meditation that it "is a practice — such as mindfulness, or focusing the mind on a particular object, thought or activity — to train attention and awareness and achieve a mentally clear and emotionally calm and stable state."

So, you do not have to focus on emptying your mind. If the purpose of meditating is to train your attention and awareness, you can do that while focusing on anything, especially while opening yourself to connect with it.

Today, if it resonates with you, deepen your connection and your awarenesses of the sensory language within your body. This is where you will find access to amazing new powers.

You have to go through the channels within the body to connect to your

Higher Self, your innate awareness, all the information streaming in through your biological centers that interact with energy, life force and Source. All these connections can bring you greater peace, health, clarity, self acceptance and knowledge of whether you are in the right place at the right time or not.

Quieting the mind and opening ourselves up to our internal and external worlds (however we achieve this) is a beneficial practice because it brings greater clarity to our inner listening and the messages that are contained therein.

One easy technique (and probably our favorite) for meditation is to connect to nature. Find a place to sit comfortably and open yourself like a flower to the living energies around you.

What visits you? What is the quality of that visit? Is it simply visiting with you, being sociable, or does its presence carry a message for you?

As your practice deepens, the experiences such encounters in nature bring you will be more and more rewarding. It can also lead to developing Whispering skills, which will enrich the experience of connecting, which in turn is so nourishing.

Anything can be a meditation and anything can be a prayer. Experiment with this and record your findings in your journal. If nothing else, simply sitting still long enough for your inner knowledge to catch up to you will reveal surprising wisdom. Remember, your path, your struggles and your successes may well be lifelines for others waking to all of this in the not-too-distant future.

Notes

Raising Our Frequency

Many things are influencing the shift in energies around us at this time: unusual planetary alignments, the precession of equinoxes, massive solar flares, coronal mass ejections (CMEs) and more. Our planet is being bombarded with high-frequency energies. These incoming energies are activating and guiding us to manifest the New Earth Consciousness for the human collective.

For us to align with the new energies it is imperative that we shed older and denser energies and raise our spiritual vibrations. We do this in many different ways. A powerful way to increase your vibration is by laughing out loud. Laughter truly is the best medicine! Another way to raise your vibration is by spending time focusing on your gratitude practice. When you are focused on being grateful, your vibration increases. Focusing on or steeping yourself in what brings you joy or what you love raises your vibration. Creating art, taking a walk in nature, yoga, singing, petting a puppy, hugging — all of these increase your vibration. Making a habit of participating daily in such practices will change your life in good ways and help you handle the shifting energetic tides around you more easily. This is why Lightworkers are constantly being reminded to practice self care.

CHANGES TO OUR WORLD

The presence of these higher frequencies in our environment brought on by both astrological and astronomical events is shifting the electromagnetic balance of the earth. All these things combined are causing those among us who are sensitive to feel disconnected from our older ways of surviving and stimulating us to want to change our place of work and even our friends. Frequencies that are not appropriate to the new paradigm become something we wish to move away from. This can be experienced as a tower moment (tarot reference), as though the world we had drawn close to us (in order to survive) is going up in flames.

WHAT WE CAN DO

This is where being able to trust your inner senses becomes crucial because, if you have not experienced that internal connection to your guidance, you will likely be aware only of the destruction, loss and grief. However, if you can touch your inner knowing, you will receive supportive information from these situations as well. Thousands of people all over the world are going through this right now.

The change in the frequencies is altering many of us, without our conscious volition. For example, are you experiencing a growing discontent with your current profession? How about your friendships? The higher vibrations of light and consciousness bathing the earth are illuminating these aspects of your life as ones that need to shift.

SHADOW SELF

The term Shadow Self refers to all the parts of us that we try to hide, suppress or are not proud of. If we are taught that it is not becoming for a young lady to get angry, what do we do with our anger? It can become relegated to a Shadow Self to carry. Trauma, repressed emotions, stifled thoughts, resentment or anger can all lead to the development of intense Shadow Selves. They are quite capable of holding onto resentment, let's say, and then when you're in a position that the Shadow Self feels like it can get away with doing so, it darts in and bombs a situation (or person) with a stinky blob of constipated emotions. If it's a clever Shadow Self, it can even make sure that it deploys this bomb in an appropriate situation.

Did I mention that these Shadow Selves operate below our conscious awareness? So when one of our Shadows goes out on a raid, we know nothing about it. It is also common for us to be in denial of our Shadow Selves.

Shadow Selves can be parts of us that felt victimized as children, and those parts may react to new situations with the pattern of feeling victimized — even if we now have power .

SHADOW WORK

Working with these unacknowledged parts of ourselves is called Shadow Work, and that is too lengthy a subject to get into now. There is much written about it, and it is very valuable work for us to do. Very valuable, but it takes courage, strength and persistence.

Do not be surprised if you are experiencing an increase in negative self-talk, self-sabotaging habits or seeing Shadow sides of yourself now. All of these are coming to light to give you the opportunity to release them. This is all part of ascension. Not fun, we know, yet the outer circumstances causing these internal changes are also affecting how quickly we can move, once and for all, through these old patterns that no longer serve us. So there are many rewards to doing this work.

Surrender

The energy of surrender is a feminine force. Surrendering is letting go of control. The need to control one's life comes from a place of fear and lack — both of which are extremely dense energies. The ego (programmed with personal, generational, and collective trauma) believes that nothing will succeed without its influence. This is far from the truth of our Universe as there is no ego that exists in the soup of God.

If we knew for certain why we are here and what our relationship to God and our destiny was, it would make sense for us to try to control our lives, down to the tiniest detail. But we don't really know any of those things, do we?

A life lived well is more about balance, isn't it? It involves finding comfortable ways to open up to the guidance and flow of life that is all around us.

Humans often have the need to try to control the outcome of situations. Al-

though it may seem to be a smart thing to do, if you really think about it, it isn't. We would have to know all the possible miracles and minutiae of each road taken or rejected in order to be successful.

But as I said, we don't. However, God, our Higher Self, our guides and other helpers do. So living life in a manner that allows for inspired guidance seems to make much more sense.

What does surrender mean to you? Have you ever experienced surrender as a superpower? What does it feel like to you? Take a moment to lean into that.

Operating from the limited perception of our ego is a sure way of keeping our spiritual vibration low, as it cuts us off from cosmic support. Each one of us has a Spirit Team that will guide us whenever we ask them to step in. All that is required from us is to choose to surrender to their love.

In truth, whenever we use one of our biological systems to read and interact with energy, we must surrender the ego and let ourselves be guided by something else — a higher source of guidance.

Trust

"There is not a human heart that exists, that if assured of safety, would not open immediately"

Trust does not spontaneously appear. Don't confuse trust with faith. Trust, like a flower, grows *if* the right nurturing and harmonious energies are present. In order to trust anything, we need multiple encounters with it. And each encounter is informed by the previous one.

You are precious. Do not trust anything until it has given you plenty of reason to do so. And even then continue to let your experience of it inform you.

Trust is understanding and relying on the capabilities of something or someone. It is built upon honest communication and keeping our promises. It is the glue that holds our relationships together.

In addition, always be mindful of those who place trust in you, because it is a sacred honor.

Remember that Don Miguel says in his book *The Four Agreements* that one should:

"Be impeccable with your word"

It is one of the most important practices we can focus on. Adhering to this can and will change your life!

TRUSTING THE PROCESS

Having said that, being able to trust the process of ascension (as it takes us through many highs and lows) takes experience, patience, and surrender.

Often we are guided through changes and shifts that our ego struggles to accept and make sense of. Remembering that we are always where we need to be can bring a lot of grace and ease into our journey.

TRUSTING THE SELF

Self-trust seems to rely upon knowing your process, which takes time. You can only trust yourself when you witness yourself reliably do certain things. When you consistently see yourself move towards the light, no matter how infinitesimally, you can truly begin to trust yourself (if growing towards the light is important to you).

Practicing being impeccable with your word is one of the fastest ways to not only develop self-trust, but also self-respect — which is one of the best feelings in the world!

Gratitude

Did you know that gratitude is one of the most powerful forces on the planet? When we focus on what we are grateful for, it instantly raises our vibration, which puts us in a more powerful place as Lightworkers.

What we focus on grows. Practicing gratitude is a sure way to focus our energy on the positive aspects of our lives and give them more power.

Our brain filters information according to our dominant thoughts (and vibrational energy). This is known as the Baader-Meinhof phenomenon. When we are grateful for the blessings, support and opportunities in our lives, we condition our brain to notice and recognize more blessings and abundance. Moreover, doing so reduces our chances of brooding over perceived misfortunes or even paying too much attention to any sort of negativity.

By being focused on the good, we see and attract more good.

Because of this, a gratitude practice is capable of changing our lives for the better. To discover this for yourself, all you have to do is practice gratitude daily for a month.

One of the easiest ways to do this is to create a gratitude list. No matter how bad things may seem, find at least one thing for which you can feel grateful each day and write it in your journal. We know this can be hard sometimes. We have all been in a place of such internal darkness that we do not feel as if there are any blessings in our lives at all. When we are feeling seriously depressed, for instance, the very thought of trying to find gratitude can seem an impossible task, one that may bring up anger. If you are experiencing this, go back to a time when you were grateful for something. If you cannot find this in your life, then imagine a scenario where you would feel grateful and spend as much time there as you can. What we focus on grows.

If things are not so bad, come up with several things you are grateful for.

When we start our day with gratitude, we set ourselves up to attract more to be grateful throughout the day. Stepping into the frequency of gratitude drives away energies of worry, lack, and fear.

Practicing gratitude is one of the most powerful and effective ways to raise our spiritual vibration.

At the end of the day, recite the things on your list. Jot down any reactions you have to this practice as the days go by. And be sure to add any new things you are grateful for.

Remember that often our most powerful lessons are ones that are uncomfortable to go through. The greater the resistance, the more the impact of the lesson (if we can grasp it). When we get to the point where we can feel grateful for a hardship because of the subsequent growth, strength or awareness it brought us, then we know we are well on our way to being gratitude masters.

Notes

Protecting Our Light

Protecting our light used to be a lot more difficult than it is now. This was partially due to the larger ratio of dark to light on the planet. Lightworkers who could see such things have described pockets of light on a mostly dark world, but this was before 2012. No longer is that the case.

We have struggled so hard to get to where we are — a planet whose consciousness is rising. The percentage of light on earth now far outweighs the dark. Did you know that? You might not have, but I want you to focus on it. Can you feel it? Many can, although they didn't think to look for it.

Celestial support, oneness, the love of God: all these things can be experienced much more easily now!

Just as many of us have not taken the time to tune in and feel this change consciously, the proponents of darkness are not necessarily aware of this yet either. The change caught everyone by surprise; it is a milestone worked toward for a very, very long time, and suddenly attained.

Consequently, we can expect that folks who are invested in the old paradigm of profiting off others' suffering will fight to maintain their access to such darkness.

They will believe that they can restore the old balance of power and they will try. But do not worry, they cannot — because this shift cannot be undone.

It is done — our very DNA is being rewritten, the quota of light on the planet is rising daily, and the only thing that blocks our access to this light is ... ourselves. Ironic, isn't it? So how do we protect and grow our light?

As light and energy workers, we have relied heavily on the traditional methods for protecting our energy (see the Energetic Cleansing section of this book). However, in the increasing light frequencies bathing the planet these days, you may find that you can shield yourself with only a thought.

As with cleansing, initially it's a good idea to get into the habit of creating some sort of intentional protection around you whenever you are going to be experimenting with energy work. It's just good practice.

After you are confident in your ability to read energy accurately, you can use your intuition as to whether something needs protection and/or cleansing.

Increasing our light is done through nurturing anything but fear within us. Fear causes us to shut down our internal light production. This is why fear was employed so often in the old paradigm.

We don't need fear now. Take deep breaths, hold yourself, let God or Source, the angels, your ancestors, guides and helpers hold you.

Love yourself into your highest vibration and shine!

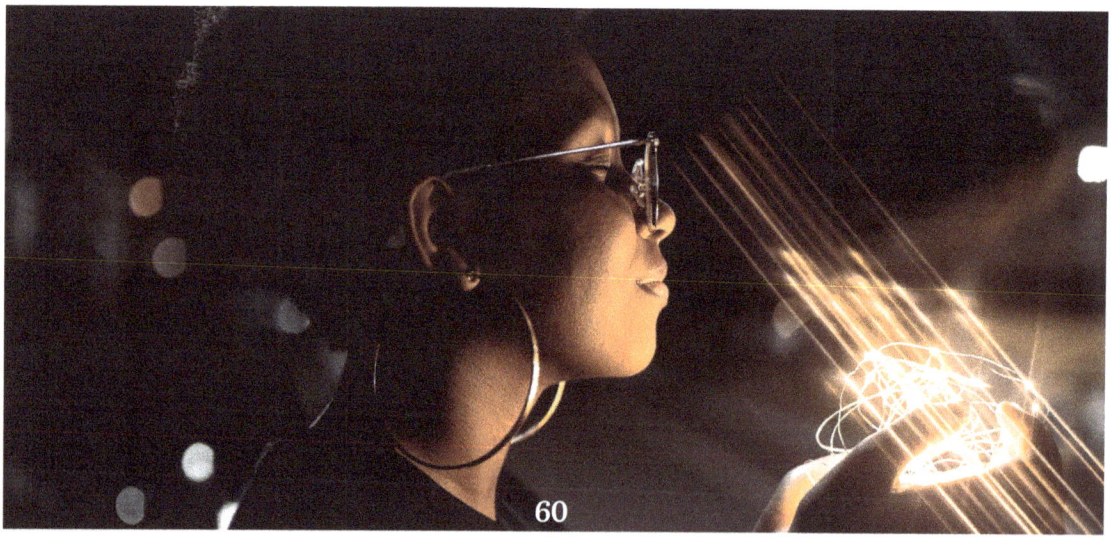

Prayers, Ancestors, Angels & Allies

PRAYERS

Even if you are not a true believer, prayers that have been said over and over again pick up great power. I (Lia) have used the Lord's Prayer in several instances with amazing results (even though a traditional concept of God is not really in my wheelhouse).

ANCESTORS

Using whatever prayers you are familiar with that ask for protection should work well. Many Indigenous teachers will tell you that knowing what your ancestors believed and practiced is very important. So looking at practices from regions where your ancestors hailed from can be rewarding.

If the practices that you are able to identify do not resonate with you, it may be that most of your past lives were in a different culture, perhaps even multiple ones. In this case it is important to use your inner guidance in picking which practices to work with. You may also find that what really resonates with you is more of an off-planet connection. The soul is ageless, its nature is unified love … it may be that only this universal vibration resonates with you. Exploration will reveal much to you.

ANGELS

Most of us are familiar with angels. Biblically they are seen as supernatural spiritual beings that serve God and act as intermediaries between God and humans, sometimes as protectors or guides for humanity. In a more modern view, angels are ancient higher dimensional beings that assist us from other realms, from maintaining the magnetic balance on the planet (or adjusting it, as is happening now to support our conscious evolution — commonly referred to today as Ascension). Depending on your perspective the latter may be harder for you to accept.

If that is you, think of it this way. The world we live in extends well beyond the spectrum visible to us. The are millions of energies, entities and entire worlds that exist alongside our reality. Many of those energies or entities are constantly in service of the conscious Ascension of humanity. You may call upon these benevolent forces to protect, guide or support you in any way that you need.

ALLIES

Allies are anything from Jungian archetypes to stones, terrestrial creatures (plant, insect, amphibian, fish, mammal or avian), disembodied spirits, magical or mythical creatures (fairies, nymphs, dryads, gnomes, elves, etc.), elementals, aliens or ancestors. Any of these can share their medicine with us or become our allies either briefly or for our entire lives. Medicine is a physical or spiritual strength, skill, or asset that can be shared with another. Some of these allies can be experienced in the form of Animal Totems or they can appear as Guides. Exploration and discernment are what is needed here, until you have a body of experience that will guide you in deepening your relationship with all these.

Crystals and Stones

The molecular structure of crystals is responsible for everything unique about them. Their molecules are more coherent, having less entropy than any other material on our planet, (because they are formed from one molecular structure repeated in a lattice). This orderly structure causes the same vibrational frequency to be repeated and amplified through repetition. So crystals' structure produces the purest frequency of any natural material.

Structure determines a crystal's type (ruby, emerald, diamond, quartz, etc.). Each type of crystal has a specific shape and color because of its molecular structure. These physical expressions of frequency can help us understand how to work with individual crystals. For example, the color of a crystal can be used to decide where on the body it can be helpful (think chakras and their associated colors).[1]

Here is one example. Black absorbs all colors, and black stones are known to absorb negative energy. Therefore all black stones can be used to help protect you, but each of them does it a little differently. Also, because they absorb negative energies, they need to be cleansed more often than other stones.

[1] For more information about stones for protection, visit www.connectingthedots.guru.

Salt, Symbols, Sigils, Talismans, Oils and Herbs

Traditionally, many substances and symbols have been used for protection.

SALT

Placing small open containers of salt (or saltwater) above doors and windows will banish and keep out unwanted energies. Creating an "energetic boundary" by pouring tiny piles of natural salt into all four corners (or directions) of a room after smudging will serve the same purpose.

You may cast a protective circle by pouring a ribbon of salt around yourself or an object (and be sure to connect the beginning to the end of the ribbon to form a circle).

The shape of the circle is sacred in many cultures, having neither a beginning nor an end. The planets are round and they travel in circles. Life is seen as a circle from birth to death. Trace a circle clockwise to build energy and counterclockwise to dissipate it.

Drawing a circle of salt around you will block anything from getting to you, just as pouring a ring of salt around an object will keep the energy of the object within the circle.

Placing salt above your doors and windowsills keeps out negative spirits. Placing a small dish of salt in the corners of your room is also good and can be combined with the previous method to augment the protection.

SYMBOLS
Our thoughts are electrical impulses jumping from synapse to synapse; our thoughts are energy, energy is powerful, and what we focus our energy on becomes both what we send out and what we attract. (It's the same thing with accumulated or intense feelings.) Symbols have accumulated power. You can utilize this energy in your work. Tune into the energy you pick up from different symbols. Use the ones that resonate with you. Experiment.

Remember that your personal associations (particularly if they are strong) will amplify your focused energy. This will flavor or color your work. It is very possible for your association to override the collective association for a particular symbol.

SIGILS
These are symbols specifically used in magic, which represent various deities. They draw energy from both their origins and associations.

They also have accumulated power derived from centuries of use.

TALISMANS
These are objects that carry a protective medicine or magic within them. They may be collectively recognized like a rabbit's foot, or they may be very personal.

Talismans can be natural objects, like the rabbit's foot, or they may be created by combining different components based on an object's properties, its symbology, its intuitively derived purpose, or personal associations.

OILS
Depending on what they are made from, oils be applied topically, eaten, used in a diffuser or worn in an amulet. Their purpose will generally be derived intuitively, from personal experience or from collective association.

HERBS
Like the oils that can be derived from them, all herbs have natural properties that can be called upon. Combining herbs with with any of the techniques mentioned above will augment their effectiveness.

Notes

Embracing Our Soul

Learning to survive in the old paradigm was quite challenging. In order to be accepted by a society deeply rooted in outdated ideals (hierarchy, competition, separation, exploitation, and manipulation), unawakened or uninitiated lightworkers paid a heavy price. Many of us had to deny and hide the quirky, odd, and powerful parts of ourselves and embody a false personality in order to feel safe and survive in a world of conformity.

However, a new energy is seeking expression on Earth, one that resonates with the vibrations of love, benevolence, cohesion, compassion, and harmony. The new consciousness is expressing itself through those brave and enduring souls who are choosing to go against the grain, question the prevalent dysfunction in society, and follow their beautiful hearts.

We are being called to do this. Any and all attempts to defy our soul's purpose and the blueprint that we came here to share with others leaves us confused, clueless, and hurt.

Yet when we came to this planet, we didn't remember any of this. We set out to navigate our families and our cultures, but little by little the act of trying to fit in shaves off parts of ourselves. The parts we lose touch with are awareness of our divinity and our constant connection to Source. We lose sight of our inner knowledge and the intimate connection with our beautiful, wise bodies. We forget how to find answers from within ourselves, because we are taught that we know nothing and must look to others for guidance. Everything that is uniquely, intimately us is soon forgotten in our desire to fit in, be accepted, please authority figures and survive.

And usually, by the time we are old enough to step out on our own, most of our awareness of our gifts and our true nature (like our eternal place in the soup of God) is blocked from our consciousness. Any time we catch glimmers of it, those same families and cultures attempt to reinforce their belief in our diminished states.

Remember —
connection dissolves addiction.

We may not be aware of of this, except that it torments us to unquestioningly accept a reality that does not resonate with us and we feel pulled towards something different ... even if it feels impossible to attain.

Have you ever asked yourself:
- Why am I so different?
- Why can't I just be like them?

This is a common theme among old souls and Lightworkers, and the answer may surprise you. It's because you are special, unique, and unprecedented. Your old, wise, and divine soul has come to Earth during this crucial time to help humanity achieve a greater expression (or experience?) of existence.

And while the old world may never be at ease with you, the New Earth welcomes you ... it needs you.

This may be hard to believe at first, perhaps because you were repeatedly told that you were useless or worse.

Nevertheless, when you choose to take that leap of faith and express your authentic vibration, you can expect the universe to support you, possibly in some miraculous ways.

Choice?

The concept of every soul having a plan in each lifetime is not new. If we are spiritual beings in a physical body, then the important question would be: "Why?"

We need to think about the reason a powerful disembodied spirit might choose to incarnate in physical form. What might be gained from this constrained and often challenging experience?

The body is a vehicle of incredible awareness and sensitivity.

Feelings from joy to agony, love to hate, passion to apathy — all these polar opposites are experienced by us via the body. So there must be some value in experiencing these things.

If the soul is evolved or enhanced in some way by experiencing the gamut of physical life, then it is reasonable to consider the possibility that each hardship, joy, pain, and pleasure is chosen for the end results that we (while in bodies) may not be conscious of.

As we age, it is often possible to look back over the course of our life and see patterns that produce consistent, specific results. Repetitive pains cause us to turn inward and perhaps develop sensitivities or gifts that we would not have otherwise. In this light it seems reasonable that we choose these things because of the potential benefits.

For example, what if we choose the families that we are born into? If your childhood was painful, it might be hard to contemplate that you would ever choose this. But there is evidence to suggest this is exactly what happens. Because we have the power to transform energies, we may also choose to be born into certain families to help them clear their ancestral lineage.

Or we may choose isolation, specific handicaps, or even trauma because of the specific gifts that have the potential to develop under those circumstances. Financial, mental, emotional, or physical challenges in life cause both a predictable range of reactions and certain strengths or mindsets to overcome them. These, in turn, will create new pathways in our consciousness that may be desirable either in this lifetime or in a future one.

If there is reincarnation, then a very long-range set of goals in conscious development makes much sense. For example, a lifetime where we experience setbacks due to a physical or mental handicap will most likely cause us to develop empathy for others who try but are not always able to succeed.

If you can embrace this perspective, then you will perceive all the roads you travel as enhancing you. It will also change how you experience other people's chosen paths. It takes us from feeling victimized by life to feeling empowered and supported by it.

Working for the Collective

If we are spiritual beings in physical bodies by choice (as discussed above), then we have to consider that we chose the situations that we must deal with while we inhabit those bodies.

TRANSMUTING FAMILY TRAUMA

If we choose the lives we are born into, there is also a possibility that we choose to take on extra baggage because we are strong enough to process it and transmute it for a particular family line, or for the larger collective.

DISSOLVING OLD PATTERNS

Remember: what we hold in our thoughts and minds becomes our reality. The patterns that we dissolve and restructure within our subconscious (while overcoming our personal hardships) are then available to the larger collective. By freeing ourselves from the old paradigm of fear, lack, and inauthenticity we empower a million others to do the same.

TRAILBLAZING

Think of the trailblazer who cuts the first swath through a dense jungle. Once the path is made, it is easier for the next person to travel. Sometimes we will work on widening narrow paths that need to become highways for humanity. It is possible to get a sense of this by self-observation.

For example, those of us who came with very different beliefs from those of our families and chose a lifestyle that doesn't align with their inherited traditions are quite possibly here to free the family from generational curses and create abundance. Think about this: all ancestors who had to deny their true identity and desires in order to avoid persecution and survive in an intolerant paradigm would stand behind such individuals, giving them strength and guidance from the spirit realms. There is a Lakota saying:

We are the answer to our ancestors' prayers.

ANIMISTS

The same would be true for those who lean into belief systems rooted in mysticism and Nature worship (such as Paganism, Wicca and Shamanism) despite being conditioned in orthodox religious cultures. These rebels, contrary to the accusations levied at them, bring pride and joy to their (spiritual) ancestors by reaching out to Mother Earth and finding their own way to understand God.

OUR MISSION

Many Lightworkers came here with the mission to shine their light of wisdom and use their powerful voices to liberate the imprisoned minds of others. These revolutionaries talk openly about taboos, debunk myths, discourage biases, and introduce new thoughts and concepts.

BEING OF SERVICE

This is a lifetime of being in divine service. We are here to raise our vibration, express our authentic selves, create abundance, enjoy bliss, and uplift each other. Lightworkers are here to show others how it is done.

Processing for the Collective

Powerful Empaths, Telepaths, Mediums and Healers, for example, often process thoughts, emotions or cosmic energies for those around them or for the collective. They do this because they are strong enough to withstand powerful, often painful or overwhelming feelings. They are masters who are able and willing to transmute these intense energies, knowing they are helping their soul families to heal and progress further on their paths.

The hardest part often is realizing that processing for more than just yourself is even a possibility.

Empaths who are involved in this process, but who cannot remember that they've "got this," often feel like life hates them. They can feel as if they are under a never-ending onslaught, moving from one intense scenario to another. This is why self-awareness and knowledge are so vital to our functioning as Lightworkers.

Keeping in mind that you may be processing for more than yourself can be a huge relief.

We Are All in This Together

Although the nature of our work as Lightworkers can be (and certainly in the past has been) isolating, the truth is we are not, and never have been, cut off from our Source.

The illusion that we are cut off has been in place to foster the development that it took to get us to this point. In order to obtain the greatest benefit from our experiences here, we needed to believe that this was the only reality. However, this illusion is no longer necessary.

Our jobs now are:

1. Embody our light, which is generated within us. As we raise our vibration (for example, by practicing gratitude) we hold and project more light.

2. Divest ourselves of limiting beliefs imposed on us by the old paradigm.

3. Begin to hold ourselves to the standards required by love, tolerance, beneficence, unity, and oneness. In other words, we need to begin to practice the principles that are to become our new paradigm.

4. Increase our self-care.

It is now possible, more than ever, to feel Source's love for us. Our light has grown and is growing to the point where many of us will no longer need to shield ourselves or cleanse our environments energetically, because our light/presence by itself is doing that.

We now become emissaries of light that darkness must flee before.

We are here to bring love into the world, and each of us has been created uniquely to embody different pieces of this new paradigm. We are each needed, loved, and special.

Everything we have endured was not in vain! And all that remains to do is begin to reap the rewards of this centuries-long process.

About the Authors

Lia Russ and Meghma Hira were drawn together across oceans and continents by destiny to help individuals who are beginning to explore the gifts discussed in this book to move into their gifts more quickly, with ease, grace, and loving support.

Lia has studied with elders from many nations. For over four decades she traveled the world seeking to understand what humans are, what we are capable of, and how to eliminate the blocks that hold each of us back from fully shining our light in the world.

She specializes in helping others heal, find peace with those root issues and turn them into powerful allies. If you would like to learn more about Lia and her work, she has written a best-selling book, *Connecting The Dots: Ancient Wisdom, Modern Science*, in which she reveals science-based information about our abilities to read, understand and work with energy. She explores ancient knowledge from around the world about humans' innate abilities. She demonstrates how these abilities are tied to biological systems inside us. These systems allow us to pick up, generate and direct energy. Lia establishes that the information our ancestors deduced regarding the world's mysteries was surprisingly accurate.

Lia is clairvoyant, clairaudient, claircognizant, and clairsentient. At the age of nine, she discovered that she could heal others.

Lia is dyslexic. Although her neurodivergence makes it challenging for her to operate in the everyday world, it allows her to perceive non-linear realities. It is natural for her to enter the Akashic Records and use her gifts to retrieve information for her clients.

We feel her presence as loving, nurturing guidance, uplifting us to find our gifts and truths. Lia has been referred to as a Spiritual Godmother. Her warmth and accumulated knowledge, along with her gifts, are a wonderful resource to add to your awakening process.

"Move towards your bliss" —
Meghma Hira @ego.alchemist

Growing up in a culture rich in the spiritual and metaphysical beliefs of the East didn't prevent Meghma from being devoured by the mechanical matrix. Conditioned to be the "golden child" of a middle-class family, she pursued "high-paying and reputable" jobs at software startups.

Realizing she had been lured into the illusion of clawing up the corporate food chain while the system digested her alive, came to her at a heavy cost. Now wary of superficial living and shallow ambitions that erode our youth and wit, Meghma hit the "eject button." Quitting her job in December 2021, she decided to test the powers of her mind and the Universal laws of Energy by aligning herself with her higher calling.

What she has learned in the time that has passed between then and now will change the lives of millions of tormented young lightworkers living in compelled complacency.

The divine intelligence and love that many cultures call God expresses itself, learns and loves through sentient beings such as ourselves. It places everything we need on our path and brings us to those who are in need of our light. Meghma hopes to educate, uplift, and learn from the New Earth collective that is aligning the planet to a higher frequency.

Meghma is a multidimensional woman from India who finds herself deeply grounded in mysticism, magic, and other mysteries of the Universe. This is where she feels most at home.

Although her journey was treacherous, she learned it is worth all the adventures leading to peace within.

Notes

Lightworkers Lifeline came about because of a need we recognized in untrained Lightworkers, Healers, Energy workers, the newly Awakened, those experiencing symptoms of Ascension and Starseeds.

Over and over again, we saw people in need of guidance to discover their gifts, to develop them and work with them, as well as deal with the physical and emotional overloads that these transitions can cost.

We acknowledge that we are all able to access any knowledge that we seek, without teachers or guidance. However, this method is time- and resource-consuming and does not address the questions or insecurities of a novice.

Lia awoke 50 years ago, alone, on a mostly dark planet. She is a perfect testimony that we can figure this stuff out without teachers or guidance in human form. But ask her if she wishes that there had been a Hogwarts or an experienced human she could trust to help her find her truths, and she would reply with a resounding YES!

A vast array of gifts is emerging on earth at this time. Although these gifts are diverse, humans tend to react to them in predictable ways: from feeling betrayed, to disbelief, to being displaced or dissatisfied with one's current life, work, friends, lovers, etc.

Knowing that you must do something different in your life — but not being able to get clear on what that is — can leave you feeling frustrated and inadequate.

These feelings are to be expected as one is exploring a new paradigm. Comfort with a new reality requires developing new skills and new ways of understanding the universe.

We can help individuals with all of this, and we do so with great joy!

Do You Want To Know What Lightworker Archetype You Are?

We have created an immersive questionnaire to help your answer just that!

Take our free

Lightworker Archetype Assessment

This 10- minute exploration reveals your dominant Lightworker Archetype.
It also identifies how the other archetypes and gifts manifest in your life.

Scan the QR code printed below or visit the following link to get started:

https://lightworkerslifeline.com/
home/archetype_assessment/

Photo Credits

The authors would like to thank the artists listed below who have made their work freely available.